SIM
THAILAND

ILLUSTRATED BY
IRENE SANDERSON

SIMPLE ETIQUETTE IN
THAILAND

By
Derek Tonkin

Paul Norbury Publications
Sandgate, Folkestone, Kent, England

SIMPLE ETIQUETTE IN THAILAND

Paul Norbury Publications
Knoll House, 35 The Crescent, Sandgate, Folkestone,
Kent, England CT20 3EE

First published 1990
© Paul Norbury Publications 1990

All rights reserved. No part of this publication may be reproduced stored in a retrieval system, or transmitted in any form or by any means without prior permission from the publishers.

ISBN 0-904404-76-5

British Library Cataloguing in Publication Data
Tonkin, Derek *1929–*
  Simple etiquette in Thailand.
  1. Thailand. Etiquette
  I. Title
  395.09593

  ISBN 0-904404-76-5

Distributed in the USA & Canada by:
THE TALMAN COMPANY, INC
150 Fifth Avenue
New York, NY 10011

Photoset in Souvenir Light 11 on 12pt
by Visual Typesetting, Harrow, Middlesex
Printed in England by BPCC Wheatons Ltd, Exeter

Contents

1 The Land *7*

2 The People *11*

3 Social Relations *17*

4 Food & Eating Out *26*

5 Business & Entertainment *32*

6 Travelling in Thailand *38*

7 The Thai Language *44*

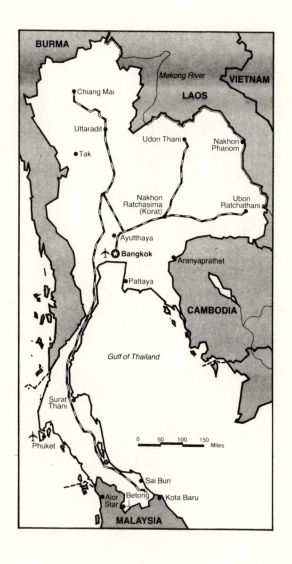

1

The Land

We used to know Thailand as 'Siam.' The country changed its name in 1939, reverted to Siam again for a brief period after the Second World War, but changed back permanently to Thailand in 1949.

The Thais themselves have called their country, in their own language, 'Thai-land' (*muang thai*, more formally *prathet thai*) for many centuries but Siam (*sayam*) has also been used as the formal name as well. Thailand, which means literally 'Land of the Free', is now the only correct international name, but Siam still appears in royal titles and in the names of some banks, companies and newspapers.

NOTE: 'Thailand' was devised just before the Second World War when Thai nationalism was particularly strong. Most scholars say that the term 'Siam' (possibly related to 'Shan' — Shan States in Burma) was a word originally used by Thailand's neighbours (Chinese, Burmese, Khmers) to describe Thailand. But some scholars have recently argued that Siam is, after all, a good Thai word.

Thailand's neighbours include Burma to the West, Laos to the North, Cambodia to the East and Malaysia to the South. Thailand, situated in the Tropic of Cancer, is about the size of France, but has almost the same population as Britain - about 55 million. There are four main regions: the North - mountainous, cool in the winter and home to numerous non-Thai hill tribes; the North-East - an arid plateau bordered to the East by the River Mekong; the Centre - a fertile rice-growing region around Bangkok; and the South - rich in rubber, tin and lush vegetation.

Visitors to Thailand should be aware of a unique feature of the country's history: it was never colonised by any western country. Over the centuries the Thais did battle with their neighbours, notably the Burmese and the Khmers (Cambodians). But from the thirteenth century onwards the Thais created a nation state which has survived intact to this day. Thailand came under some pressure from western trading nations in the seventeenth century. Two centuries later, during the hey-day of colonial expansionism, the British in Burma and Malaya and the French in Laos and Cambodia secured significant concessions in territory as well as trade. But the Thais, under the wise leadership of King Mongkut (Rama IV), 1851-1868, and King Chulalongkorn (Rama V), 1868-1910, succeeded where almost all other South-East Asian nations failed, in preserving their independence.

This absence of a colonial past (though Thailand made sensible use of the services of numerous western advisers, particularly from France, Britain and Germany) is important to an understanding of Thai mentality. Thais have no chips on their shoulders. Visitors are welcomed as equals. Racial and religious prejudice is virtually unknown. Buddhist tolerance goes hand in hand with intense national pride. Poised to become the next NIC (Newly Industrialising Country) in the Asia-Pacific Region, Thailand has the natural and human resources both to enjoy the benefits of industrialisation and to preserve its traditions and culture, blessed as it is with an economy balanced between light industry, agriculture and services.

Thailand's principal exports have been rice, rubber, manioc and canned foods, but in recent years manufactured products have overtaken traditional agricultural produce and

---

NOTE: In 1782 the crown was offered to one of King Tak Sin's generals, Chao Phraya Chakri who was crowned with the title of Rama I. The present monarch is HM King Bhumibol Adulyadej, the ninth monarch in the Chakri Dynasty, or Rama IX. (Many Thai kings have used the name 'Rama' derived from the name of the hero of the Indian epic Ramayana. Rama was the archetype of the perfect ruler. The system of designating monarchs in the present Chakri Dynasty as 'Rama' was created by King Vajiravudh, who became Rama VI. He renamed all previous monarchs Ramas I - V).

include jewellery, integrated circuits, textiles and footwear. Thailand now exports bicycles to Britain and motor-cars to Canada.

Overseas visitors, especially those from the West, are known to the Thais as *farangs*. The word is most probably a corruption of 'Frank' and originally meant Caucasians from the ports of the Near East (and not 'French,' as is popularly believed). It is also, fortuitously, the Thai word for the guava fruit. As a guava/farang in Thailand, you can never escape your western origins. Yet there are, inevitably, those earnest young westerners on a longish stay in Thailand who desperately wish to assimilate and become indistinguishable from their Thai hosts. I wonder why. As a six-foot, blue-eyed blonde Scandinavian, you are never going to merge with the local Thai population. The Thais much prefer you as you are.

Two golden rules for visitors to Thailand. First, always show proper respect for the Thai monarchy; never make derogatory remarks, it could land you in real trouble, for Thais are intensely proud of their national heritage and Royal Family. Second, behave modestly and sensibly in all matters relating to the Buddhist religion, especially when visiting temples; Buddhism is the guiding influence in the Thai character, as you will learn in the following pages. I should add that Thai temples are externally very photogenic, but do be careful when photographing inside temples in case there are restrictions.

2

The People

Thailand was settled over the centuries by waves of migration, including Khmers and Mons (from Burma) and various peoples from southern China. The Thais arrived from Yunnan in southern China in the tenth and eleventh centuries and by the thirteenth century had established the first Thai capital at Sukhothai, moving to Ayutthaya in the fourteenth century and to Bangkok in the eighteenth century.

Most Thais live in the countryside. A typical rural family will include grandparents, cousins, an uncle or aunt, even children of distant relatives. Living together under one roof encourages natural courtesy, tolerance and mutual respect, in the interests of social harmony. Urban households retain these traditional values, as far as practicable; invariably, there are relatives up-country and so most urban Thais retain, and enjoy, their links with the countryside.

From an early age, Thais are brought up to accept a code of social behaviour based on respect for superiors, parents, teachers and the elderly. Accordingly, the emphasis in relationships tends to be vertical, rather than horizontal; deference, avoidance of conflict, a desire to please are hallmarks of the Thai character. This has in the past encouraged patronage and limited the scope for advancement by merit. But as Thailand progresses economically and a sophisticated, urbanised population emerges, opportunities for personal advancement, particularly in the private sector, are bound to expand.

The Buddhist religion has been a dominant influence, probably the most important factor, in the development of the Thai personality. Thai village life over the years has followed a cyclical pattern of farming which is reflected in a cycle of fixed Buddhist festivals throughout the year. In its purest form, Buddhism is a religion of simplicity and quiet contemplation. The Buddha, which means simply 'The Enlightened One,' was a prince who lived in Northern India 25 centuries ago (1990 AD is Buddhist Era [BE] 2533); he renounced material comforts in the search for enlightenment about the nature of human existence. In Thailand, Buddhism was enhanced by Brahminism, which brought colour, festivity and ritual to the religion and gave the Thai people a pleasantly practical interpretation of the Buddha's teachings.

On the whole, Thais are content to accept their lot without carping or resentment, though their approach to life is invariably positive, carefree and good-natured. There is perhaps a certain fatalism in their attitude, deriving from the Buddhist concept of 'karma,' which basically means 'action;' the law under which your present life is determined by the cumulative merit of previous existences, and though materialist influences have in recent years had some impact, most Thais prefer a life of contentment and enjoyment to one of material acquisition.

Buddhism teaches that life is suffering, that earthly pleasures are only transient and that progress towards enlightment and the attainment of eventual 'nirvana' (salvation) requires personal commitment. The acquisition of merit through good deeds helps to this end. Thais do not believe, however, that life should be taken all that seriously. As farmers, Thais know that rice cultivation is strenuous work and that life would not be all that much fun without some diversion and communal jollity. Ploughing, seeding, transplantation and harvesting would certainly be tedious without having a laugh. Work and play do indeed mix in Thailand, so much so that the word for work *ngarn* is also the word for festival or fair; the common meaning is communality.

One of the first words you will learn in Thai is *sanuk* (pronounced sa-nook), which roughly translated means fun. No activity in Thailand is thought worth undertaking unless it is *sanuk*. When a friend tells you what he has been up to, you are almost expected to ask *Sanuk mai?* or 'Was it fun?'. The Thai life-style, whether in the town or the country, is geared to pleasurable activities. A night out with friends, a trip up-country, a visit to relatives, a walk to a temple at festival times are all likely to be *sanuk*.

As activity frequently involves travel, another essential Thai expression is *bpai tiao* (pronounced by-tiaow, as in 'miaow'), which literally means 'to go on a trip'; we would say 'going out.' Thais love travel, whether short or longish journeys, since travel involves socialising, seeing new faces, meeting up with old friends. An evening at the cinema, a walk across the fields, a visit to a fair, are typical examples of *bpai tiao* which can also cover chatting up the girls and a night out on the town. *Bpai tiao* is, by definition, almost certain to be *sanuk*.

Another strong influence on the Thais is the unknown, the supernatural, the world of spirits. Thais have a strong sense of the inexplicable, an acute awareness of the mystery of nature. The clearest manifestation of this are the gaily-coloured spirit houses which grace most gardens and households and places of natural beauty or ominous interest like an outcrop of rocks near a temple or an accident-prone locality on a highway. The local guardian spirits are there by natural right; people are only incidental occupants of land and property and need to respect, and occasionally humour, the local spirits. In daily life, many Thais take care not to upset the spirits who are thought to be born out of the souls of departed human beings. Some spirits are perceived more as ghosts (called *pee*), unpredictable and malevolent, the source of misfortune and chicanery, the cause of terror, illness and material loss. In north-east Thailand, spirit worship is especially active.

It is scarcely surprising that, in such an uncertain world, Thais take sensible precautions. As a basic rule of conduct, no human venture should be launched until the auspicious moment. No business undertaking is initiated, no marriage solemnised, no decision of substance taken until the precise time designated by astrological calculation has been reached. An invitation to the opening of a new branch office, for example, will indicate in the programme the precise minute at which the new venture will be most auspiciously launched.

Dreams, premonitions, intuitive knowledge are taken seriously. Good and bad omens are seen as portents of success and failure. Charms and amulets are worn by many Thais, the most popular type of amulet naturally being small images of the Buddha. Spells and incantations, mystic formulae and protective tattoos all help to subdue malevolent spirits, who can also be bribed to remain dormant or, temporarily, go away.

After all, since whatever you do and whatever precautions you may take may not achieve the desired result, it is better not to worry. *Mai bpen rai* or 'never mind' is heard on almost any occasion. Literally, it means 'there isn't anything' and it is a bit like the French *ce n'est rien* and the German *macht nichts*. *Mai bpen rai*, however, is used so much more frequently than equivalent western expressions that it suggests as much a state of mind, an extension of Buddhist philosophy and, to the westerner, sounds even a little exasperating. Thais have learnt to relax in times of adversity and disappointment. They do not get over-excited, for example, if the train is late or if they are stuck in a traffic jam on the way to the airport. No need to cry, better to laugh instead.

The basic social structure in Thailand is the individual family; groups of families are associated in village communities. The family represents stability and security in an ever-changing, uncertain world. Loyalty to and respect for the family, to the village, to the monarchy and to the country are highly developed. This encourages a strong sense of national identity and pride.

3

Social Relations

Thais are very sociable. You will find it fun (*sanuk*) getting to know them. But before doing so, you should try to learn something about their social codes.

Greeting

Thais greet each other very much as people do anywhere else in the world, with a cheery sign of recognition and a chat. The most usual greeting, appropriate on almost all occasions, and it is also a farewell, is *sawatdee* which literally means 'May you prosper.' It may be used at any time of the day or night. To be polite, men should add the word *krap* and women the word *ka*, so that for men it is *sawatdee krap* and for women *sawatdee ka*. *Krap* (in Bangkok often shortened to *k'ap*) and *ka*, incidentally, are the nearest words you can get in Thai to 'yes,' though they mean little more than 'I hear you.' You can also say *sabai dee*, which is closer to our 'How are you?', but not so frequent as *sawatdee* except in the north-east (and Laos).

Thais do not normally shake hands among themselves, though they will shake western hands because they know that is what foreigners do. Custom, however, is slowly changing and in recent years it has become accepted practice for Thais to shake hands among themselves on special occasions, for example, when signing commercial contracts or at prize-givings, particularly at sports meetings, where both a *wai* and a handshake are in order.

The Wai

The traditional Thai greeting, and farewell, is to raise both hands gracefully and unhurriedly, palm to palm and close to the body, in what is known as the *wai* (pronounced 'why'). It is tempting, but mistaken, to regard this as the equivalent of our handshake. In Thailand, to *wai* means not only to greet and farewell; more importantly, it means to pay your respects. The higher you raise your hands, the greater the respect you wish to convey.

The *wai* is accordingly always initiated by the person whose status, for reasons of age or rank, is inferior to the person to whom respects are being paid. When you join your Thai International flight at London Heathrow, Frankfurt, Sydney or Los Angeles, the exquisitely dressed Thai air hostess will always *wai* to you, and she will *wai* to you again when you leave the flight in Bangkok. She does not expect you to respond; a smile and a nod are all that is needed. When you arrive at your hotel, you are likely to be met with a *wai* as you enter. Again, do not try to respond; it is not expected and you will be at a loss about how to *wai* with your hands full of hand luggage.

A person who initiates a *wai* is likely to bend his head very slightly, particularly when making a *wai* to someone who is sitting or lying down. The recipient of a *wai* normally, but not always, responds with a *wai*, hands held slightly lower, head at normal height. Watch the news on TV and observe how people of various ranks and status *wai* and respond. When the gap between greeter and recipient is significant, a *wai* may be returned only with a smile or a nod. Note how members of the Thai Royal Family at religious ceremonies themselves *wai* to the Buddhist clergy and how the latter, because of their special status in society, do not themselves respond to a *wai* with any physical movement.

Practice makes perfect

If you are staying in Thailand for any length of time, you will gradually learn how and when to make a *wai*. Watch a company Chairman responding to the *wai* made simultaneously by the members of his Board of Directors with his own collective *wai* while holding a bundle of papers in his right hand and his briefcase in his left hand, but somehow contriving to bring one hand close to the other without dropping anything. See how schoolgrils *wai* and at the same time bob in a curtsy to their teachers, how peasants raise their hands up to their foreheads when greeting a member of the Royal Family, how prominent personalities when seated hold their hands in a mid-way *wai* position of quiet contemplation and reverence while listening to a Buddhist recitation.

The golden rule for newcomers is to smile at all times, *wai* only when you are quite sure it is the right thing to do and watch closely how the Thais themselves play out this age-old ritual. The most serious mistake you can make is to wave your hands around in a *wai* to all and sundry, in the mistaken belief that because you have seen something similar in India, it is alright to do the same in Thailand. Thais will be too polite and too shy to correct you; but they will laugh at you, from embarrassment, and you will make a further mistake if you interpret their laughter as pleasure and delight.

The Thai Smile

Thailand is indeed known as the Land of Smiles. In the West, we smile because we have something to smile about. In Thailand, people smile naturally, out of sheer *joie de vivre* but also because they have been brought up from an early age to please. To some extent the

Thai smile is designed to placate unknown and possibly hostile forces, particularly awkward, red-faced foreigners. So there is something defensive about the Thai smile, designed to put you at ease. Thais do smile, of course, and often laugh at jokes and comic situations, as we do in the West, but harmless personal misfortunes (like being splashed by a passing car or losing a coin down a drain) at which westerners might chuckle in private, Thais will observe with an open smile on their faces. The intention is not to laugh at you, but to help you psychologically out of your misfortune by sharing your experience and suggesting subliminally that there could be worse calamities!

From this you will gather that Thais are inclined to smile when they are embarrassed. The car behind bumps into you. You get out to remonstrate. The Thai driver is smiling. You resist the temptation to punch him on the nose. Instead, you smile back. His smile is the Thai way of saying sorry. Your smile is your acceptance of his excuses. He will smile back again to say thank you. Three smiles with three different meanings. So tempers are kept on both sides.

Some visitors conclude from all this that Thais are adept at smiling their way out of almost any situation. I suppose, in some ways, this could be true. But after all, why not? Of course, if the driver behind you is driving a truck and demolishes half your car, he is likely to conclude that no amount of smiling will cool your anger; so the chances are that he will simply take to his heels, both to avoid the police and an unpleasant confrontation with you.

Finally, you will notice that nearly all Thai girls smile at you. This is not a 'come hither' appeal (in most cases). It is their way of looking prettier. After all, you would surely prefer smiles to scowls, laughter to grumpy frowns.

Body Movements

Thais are naturally graceful and seem in perfect control of their bodies. Westerners look clumsy, ungainly, uncontrolled and even uncultured. But then Thais are taught from an early age to control their physical movements whereas the emphasis in the West tends to be on free physical expression. Thai girls are taught the elements of traditional dancing, where the main elements are poise, decorum and restraint.

Perhaps the first thing you will notice about social interreaction in Thailand is what the westerner calls 'high posture/low posture' relations. Traditionally, Thais show respect for elders and superiors by ensuring that they do not loom physically over those higher up the social ladder. So there is a lot of ducking of heads and apparent cringing, which is not cringing at all but solely a display of respect. With Thai royalty, it was standard practice to crawl in the presence of members of the Royal Family. These traditions remain in Thailand today and at all formal occasions Thais will ensure that their heads are below the level of the member of the Royal Family to whom they are speaking.

You make the greatest mistake if you interpret this formalised subservience as out of keeping with Thailand's blossoming democracy. Thais are much attached to their cultural rituals and suggestions from foreigners that such behaviour is 'undemocratic' will be dismissed out of hand.

What you do with your heads, hands and feet is therefore very important. The head (and hair) are almost sacred. The feet are profane. Pointing your feet at someone else, particularly at his head, is regarded as insolent behaviour. It is so easy to do. Try crossing your legs while sitting and you will find that one foot is pointing straight up to the head of someone sitting on the other side of the room. So when seated, try to remember not to cross your legs; worse still is to rest them on another chair or put them on top of your desk.

As for your hands, try to keep them under control. Resist the temptation to pat youngsters on the back. Pointing with fingers is not quite as bad as pointing with your feet, but control your natural (western) inclination to do so. Men should never touch women in public. Of course, times are changing and where youngsters congregate, for instance in Siam Square near Chulalongkorn University in Bangkok, you may see daring youngsters of the opposite sex holding hands. You will, alas, also see foreigners (often overweight, balding, late middle-aged westerners) holding hands with bar-girls; but that makes well brought up Thai girls even more circumspect when going out with western men.

Keeping your Temper

Buddhism is the Middle Path, the avoidance of extremes and violence, the attainment of harmony, inner and external. So Thai behaviour eschews displays of conflict and temper. Keeping a cool heart (*tjai yen*) in all possible circumstances is not only ideal behaviour but the norm. Though angry and frustrated, Thais rarely give vent to their feelings. A hot head (*tjai rawn* or hot heart) is a social lapse. Westerners are almost expected by Thais to lose their tempers at some point. Placating Thai smiles, alas, sometimes have the opposite effect. The maintenance of superficial harmony, however black your thoughts, may produce underlying psychological tensions which, when they do come to the surface, lead to violence. The Thai murder rate puts Thailand well up the international league. Avoiding conflict necessarily leads to some superficiality in contacts. Anger in any case might upset malevolent spirits.

Some Thais seem to get drunk easily, possibly because of their light body weight; but in such circumstances friends and even bystanders will try to placate the drunk or smile embarrassingly to excuse his behaviour. A drunken man is, after all, out of control. With a 'hot heart' he may (or malevolent spirits may induce him to) get up to all sorts of mischief, like tossing a hand-grenade at his rival in love, perhaps at a crowded fair-ground.

Like physical violence, verbal violence is equally unbecoming. Criticism is regarded as a form of verbal abuse. Irony and sarcasm are taboo. A dressing down, even in private, induces resentment. If behaviour is less than ideal, the vaguest of suggestions in due course about how matters might be improved is as far as most Thais would go. An employee dismissed for very good reason may harbour a grudge which could last for years and then suddenly lead to an explosion. A servant summarily dismissed for theft could lead to a male relative taking a pot-shot at you; worse, a hired gunman, who is less likely to miss, is not too difficult to find in Thailand. As a visitor, you are unlikely to find yourself in such situations. But beware of shaking off tourist and night-club touts too physically; their friends may jump on you if you react too strongly to their propositions. At all times, a smile means you know the name of the game.

Face

Much of what you have read in this chapter is about 'losing face.' Almost anywhere in the East, 'face' is important. There is probably no need to go into further detail here, except to say that Thais will go to great pains to ensure that, so far as possible, you do not lose face. It is almost as though saving the face of others is more important than the risk of losing your own.

4

Food & Eating Out

Thais love eating; indeed, they seem to spend most of their waking hours nibbling at anything that takes their fancy. With 55 million potential customers, restaurants of all shapes and sizes spring up, if needs be, overnight. Itinerant vendors, sometimes pushing a ramshackle cart or even carrying a food kitchen balanced on a bamboo pole, are everywhere. If a new building-site opens up, within 24 hours a lean-to shack restaurant will appear, as if by magic, selling noodles, curry and banana fritters. The food is good, you will see quite respectable people sitting down for their midday meal at very modest pavement kitchens, just a few wooden stools and a couple of rickety, plastic-covered tables.

Thai food has developed remarkably over the last 20 years. It was always there, of course, but it is the sheer variety which appeals to foreigners. So many rice dishes, fish and seafood in so many variations, soups which are a meal in themselves. The variety of Thai food no doubt stems from the fact that Thailand has been a crossroads of the East, with the cuisines of India, China and Malay-Indonesia making their own particular contributions.

Curiously, it is not all that easy to find really fashionable Thai food restaurants in Bangkok. They are to be found in the main international-class hotels, but tend to be a bit touristy. The *Lemon Grass*, *Bussacarum* and *Than Ying* restaurants are excellent value because they are not all that much frequented by tourists. There are some splendid restaurants on or near the Chao Phya River; and the *Tumnak Thai*, the largest restaurant in the world, is well frequented by Thais and so cleverly arranged in individual pavilions that you do not feel you are one among 3,000 guests.

Restaurants

Thais tend to eat out in groups, either colleagues at work, friends or a family gathering. No household kitchen could hope to compete with the variety available even at the most modest restaurants, so on the whole most Thais eat out most of the time, in the open air. There is a tendency for middle-class Thais to patronise Chinese restaurants, serving mostly Cantonese food. This tends to be rather bland and, for visitors to Thailand, something of a disappointment. I am a bit mystified about why Chinese food is so popular in Bangkok, when these days the Thai cuisine offers such variety. I suspect that it has something to do with the dominance of Chinese cuisine in the past, the influence of immigrant Chinese in Bangkok during the past 150 years and the social conviction that Chinese restaurants are the place to go for a good meal out.

At restaurants serving Thai food, a fork and spoon are the only eating utensils. Chopsticks are generally for use only at Chinese restaurants, though they are sometimes used for eating noodles. In village homes up-country, forks and spoons are sometimes dispensed with, the right hand being used with a lump of rice to absorb whatever food is available. In restaurants, sticky rice is most manageable with the hands. The fork and spoon you use will, incidentally, last you throughout your meal, whether the dishes change from spicy ('hot') to sweet and sour, salty or pungent. Dishes may be served piping hot, but are eaten even when cold.

Thais appreciate good food, but they do not belch or lick their fingers in public. You should begin eating as soon as the food is put in front of you; men are invariably served first. Thailand is something of a male-oriented society, in that men generally go ahead of women into lifts, restaurants and offices.

Some Thai food can be very spicy; peppers can be bad enough, but some chillies will take the roof off your mouth and bring tears to your eyes. If this happens to you, take some water and counteract the spice with plain rice or some sweet dish, even a spoonful of sugar. If you are drinking beer with your meal do not attempt to 'cool down' by drinking more of it: instead you should not touch a drop for at least five minutes!

Who pays?

If a Thai invites you to a restaurant, he will naturally expect to pay. You will notice that he does not leave a tip, except perhaps a few baht for the waitress; this is because a service charge is invariably included or assumed to be included and, in any case, tipping is not a widespread custom. If you go on a business trip to Thailand, it could be that you should pay if you are the most senior person present.

Guessing the status of other people is one of the more sensitive social preoccupations of Thais and so much depends on your assessment of the age, family connections and wealth of others present, and their assessment of you. Potentially, much 'face' is at stake, particularly if you or your colleagues get it wrong. As a person of status, you are expected to do the honours and your failure to do so, or to offer only to split the bill, will not only make you lose status in the eyes of your Thai hosts, but may cause offence as well. If you wish to retain respect, be prepared to pay as required.

From all this, you may perhaps have concluded that status and respect may be bought in Thailand. In a society where prostitution is endemic, many young women aspire to money because money brings power and power brings status. Money is the means to social redemption; the loss of face in prostitution may be more than compensated for by the acquisition of the means to improve one's status eventually.

Visiting Thai Homes

Despite the emphasis on eating out, you may occasionally be invited to a Thai home. Even in modern apartments, the rule is to take off your shoes. It is mainly a token of respect and not so much a desire, as westerners tend to assume, not to bring dirt into the household; it is also much cooler without shoes on. You will probably sit in chairs, but you might also be invited to sit on the floor. Try not to sit cross-legged; sit on your heels if you wish; better still, tuck your legs under you on one side, supporting yourself if you must with one hand. Try not to sit against a wall with your feet pointing out.

Gifts

Take a small present for your host, who may give you one in return. Flowers are always welcome, or a box of local confectionary/cookies, or some attractive small ornament: it need not be large and expensive. It is the thought that counts. Thais themselves love presents; they are often beautifully wrapped with pretty ribbon. It used to be thought bad form to open presents straight away, but this taboo is less strict nowadays and, if invited, you may take a look. On balance, though, it is better to put the present aside until later, unless you are quite sure it would not cause offence by opening it up there and then.

If you are staying overnight, spare a thought for the house spirits. There is in particular the Lord of the Place (Phra Phum) who has his shrine in the compound and there are possibly other spirits of the locality, normally at least another eight. I once slept, unawares, in a room haunted by a malevolent spirit, but as I was a foreigner, I had nothing to worry about.

5

Business and Entertainment

Business Culture

The rules about social behaviour and entertaining apply very much to business relations as well. Because Bangkok is such a sprawling metropolis and the traffic at times so exasperating that it can take you well over an hour to get across town, you will probably find that you can, with luck, make only two business calls in a morning and only one in the afternoon. This tends not to leave all that much time for entertaining your business contacts, even if you and they would like to get together.

Business lunches are very acceptable and the better-class restaurants provide a crisp, but relaxed service. As many Bangkok businessmen leave home at 6.30 or 7.00 in the morning, by 12.00 they are more than ready for their midday meal, so 1 o'clock lunches tend not to be all that welcome. Thais on the whole prefer Thai or Chinese food, but will gladly eat Western food if the opportunity occurs. Nouvelle cuisine is still very much in vogue at the top-class restaurants like the Normandie Grill in the Oriental Hotel and Le Cristal at the Regent. Low calory, salad-oriented business lunches for the health-conscious businessman are catching on only slowly.

Inviting your business contacts out to an evening meal needs careful judgement. On the whole, Thais like to get away from the office by 4.30 or 5.00 at the latest and are frankly not all that interested in hanging around in town until dinner time, which can be as early as 6.30. If your associates are sufficiently senior and westernised, they will understand the importance of relaxed entertainment when those controversial clauses in the deal under negotiation can perhaps be finally agreed. However, although they may be too polite to say so, a formal dinner is likely to be, for most except Board-level representatives, something of an ordeal. If you can contrive more informal entertainment in very casual attire (buffet dinner on a river launch, a private room in a popular restaurant), this is likely to find far greater favour with your Thai guests.

Everyone in Thailand has a business card, even the management trainees. So take a good stock with you. Some years ago it used to be fashionable to have your cards printed in Thailand in English on one side and in Thai on the other, but this practice is waning as knowledge of English increases and, frankly, is no longer either necessary or desirable. Most Thais (and even some westerners!) acknowledge that spelling in any language is only a rough guide to pronunciation, so that your English-language visiting card is adequate in itself. But do try and include as much detail as possible, including your telephone, telex, fax and even home number. It helps to build up your status and personality.

Finally, a word of advice about those special payments which some say are essential to doing business out East. Find yourself a reliable local agent and listen to his advice. Should he feel that for any reason it might be prudent to offer a special commission, technical fee, research charge, agency split or any other euphemistic payment, let him attend to this in his own way. Above all, do not yourself get involved in passing money in brown paper envelopes under the table to individuals who have somehow convinced you that the secret of success lies in their personal remuneration on the side. You will invariably pass the wrong sort of money, at the wrong time, to the wrong people. Take the perfectly respectable view that, as a westerner, you cannot possibly begin to understand these mysteries. All local firms have local fixers. Never forget that, for public-sector contracts, there is a formidable Counter-Corruption Commission which can (and does) descend on unwary public servants and take them and their books away for minute investigation. You should also know that some of the most successful western firms in Bangkok have never ever resorted to illegal payments, precisely because there are so many legal ways in which these delicate matters can be satisfactorily resolved, to everyone's mutual satisfaction.

A Night out on the Town

Thais can be very hospitable, even lavish with their entertainment, it enhances their status and they regard money spent on having fun (*sanuk*) as money well spent. They will not expect you to reciprocate in Thailand, nor to 'stand the next round.'

Bangkok's night life is world famous. Provided you watch your spending, a night out on the town can be relatively inexpensive. There are a thousand-and-one distractions for males. For couples, the flashy discos and more intimate videotheques, the jazz and dixie-land night spots, even the go-go bars can be a lot of fun. Women are welcomed, and safe, almost anywhere, but are unlikely to want to stay for the duration. As a single woman, it is best to go in company; two women can enjoy the scene, but not much else.

Most males make their way to Patpong, three street blocks in an area between Silom and Suriwongse Roads. Patpong 1 and 2 cater principally for western and English-speaking tourists, Patpong 3 for Japanese. There are a range of ground-floor bars, with gyrating go-go girls, the music not quite as ear-splitting as in the discos. The bar-girls will chat you up, but not pester you. Their English is pretty limited. You can stay for about half an hour on one beer (Baht 60) and a coke (Baht 50) or two for the girl who sits with you. [Note: The current rate is Baht 25 = $1]. You can then move on to another ground-floor bar, or venture upstairs to one of the first-floor establishments ('second floor' if ground-floor is your first floor) which have even more scantily-dressed girls and will offer floor shows as well. Prices are double, if not treble, the ground-floor establishments and what you see, particularly during the floor shows, may make your eyes pop, so I suggest that you do not go upstairs if you are easily shocked.

Apart from Patpong, there are similar complexes at Soi ('lane') Cowboy and at the Nana Entertainment complex. You might also try a massage, traditional style (perfectly respectable) or at one of the tourist massage parlours (where anything goes). The larger massage parlours along Petchaburi Road nowadays mostly cater for locals and some masseuses are reluctant to take on westerners because of growing concern about Aids.

The bar-girls and masseuses who service the tourist industry have become something of a legend. By and large, they are not the kind of toughened hustlers who operate in West European countries. Most of them come to Bangkok hoping to make about Baht 100,000 over five years, enough for them to return home up-country and open a dress-making shop or beauty salon, and hopefully to settle down and marry (a second time: their first marriage is generally disastrous, which may be why they came to Bangkok in the first place). They will laugh and cry with you, but some of them are not as sophisticated as they seem and are learning about Aids the hard way.

Dotted around Bangkok are what are described as 'Member Clubs.' These are for local businessmen, not for foreign tourists. As a casual visitor, you will pay through the nose, so do not venture inside unless you are taken by a Thai friend at his expense.

Most hotels have booklets and leaflets about places of entertainment, including tips about which restaurants, bars, discos, jazz and piano night spots are in fashion. One final word of advice: if ever you find yourself being hustled by a bar owner, do not react violently, but as soon as you get outside, ask for help from the ever-watchful Tourist Police and, without too much trouble, you will get your money back.

Travelling in Thailand

As a visitor to Thailand, you may wish to do some travelling on your own. There is an excellent domestic airline, Thai Airways, now amalgamated with Thai International, linking all the main towns in Thailand (Boeing 737s and BAe 146s). There is also a good railway network and buses and coaches of all descriptions.

Taxis

Taxis in Bangkok are cheap, usually Baht 40 (£1 or $1.60) for a short journey of 2-3 kilometres to Baht 80 or 100 for a longer trip (5 to 10 kilometres); no tip is expected. Taxis do not use meters, even if they have them installed. One experiment with meters failed some years ago and one day, no doubt, they will be tried again. 'Tuk-tuks' or three-wheeled motorised scooters are cheaper than taxis, starting at around Baht 10 for a short trip. Taxi and tuk-tuk drivers rarely speak any English and some have only the haziest notion of Bangkok's geography, possibly having only arrived that week from up-country. Better not to ask whether they are insured or have a driving licence. In the absence of meters, agree a price beforehand; some bargaining may be needed.

Cars

Cars may be hired. As in Britain (and Malaysia, Singapore, Indonesia, Hong Kong and Japan), cars drive on the left, the speed limit in towns is 60 kms an hour and 100 kms an hour in the country. After overtaking, you are expected to move back into the left-hand lane; there is generally no 'slow' lane as in Europe, unless it is specifically designated. Most road signs are in Thai, warning signs included. You may feel it better to hire a driver as well, which will only add another 25-30 per cent on the cost of the hire. If you do want to drive yourself, a valid international driving licence is required.

Be warned that up-country heavy trucks will not necessarily get out of your way on narrow roads and bus drivers sometimes race each other for fun (more *sanuk*), urged on by the passengers in both buses. There have been some appalling accidents. If you are involved in a minor accident, as a foreigner you are assumed to be richer and so are expected to pay (your higher status, hence your privilege). In more serious accidents, the other driver is likely to have the advantage of speaking fluent Thai, but he might flee the scene if he has no licence or is blatantly in the wrong.

Hire cars only from hotels and reliable agencies. Even then, check on insurance. Beware of hiring motor-cycles at holiday resorts. They may well not be insurable and could be technically defective. Sadly, many young foreigners do themselves serious injury on these contraptions.

Bangkok traffic is in no sense aggressive and Thai drivers will always let you into the main stream from a side turning. Unfortunately, while waiting for the construction of a mass transit system, the roads are overcrowded and traffic delays can be very frustrating (but keep a 'cool heart'!). Bangkok has an excellent bus system, including minibuses, ordinary buses and air-conditioned coaches. Fares are very cheap; maximum Baht 5 for 8 kms on an air-conditioned coach.

Clothing

Westerners visiting Thailand will find the climate hot and Bangkok can at times be particularly oppressive and debilitating. So clothing should be light, loose and airy. Thais are modest in clothing and most prefer to cover up against the sun when outside. Foreigners, on the other hand, tend to undress as far as they dare even in town (and at beaches more than they should). Natural fibres, such as cotton, are much to be preferred to synthetics. Most men wear short-sleeved shirts when at leisure, but long sleeves are sometimes worn in better class restaurants, where the air-conditioning can be fierce. You will rarely see Thai women with bare shoulders, and too flimsy dresses in air-conditioned establishments can ruin an evening.

It is not too difficult to spot the less culturally conscious visitor to Thailand. He could well be wearing shorts which reveal hairy legs while his chest is covered by a string singlet. His huge physical frame (occasionally with a beer belly) makes him appear slightly grotesque to Thais. On the other hand, she is wearing a mini-skirt or shorts and something rather too daring above. This lack of modesty is regarded by Thais as thoroughly bad taste. But tourism is an important money-spinner (some 5 million tourists now bring in around US$2 billion annually), so allowances are made; in any case, as a foreigner, you are likely to find yourself paying rather more in entrance fees to various establishments than the locals, an issue which gives rise to perpetual controversy in the local English-language press.

Westerners who live in Thailand for any length of time soon adapt to the sartorial customs of the country; light-weight trousers (pants) for men, sports shirts and fairly sturdy sandals. At the beaches, topless bathing is just possible in some areas (parts of Phuket and offshore islands like Ko Samui and Ko Samet), but most Thais regard it as silly; who wants to get sun-burnt and invite skin cancer? Thai girls go to great lengths to keep the sun off their skin; the paler their skin, the greater their imagined beauty.

Visiting Temples

As noted earlier, one of the most attractive features of Thai culture are the Buddhist temples to be found all over the country, even in smaller villages. In Bangkok and other towns, the temples (known in Thai as *wat*) can be very elaborate, ornate constructions. A typical *wat* normally includes a *bot* used by the monks for ordinations, a *viharn* used for public worship where the main temple images of the Buddha are normally kept and a *sala* or rest-house or pavilion. Buddha images do not represent the Buddha as a deity, but are meant to help the individual, through contemplation of the image's serenity, in his progress towards enlightenment. They are not primarily seen as works of art.

While Thais are tolerant for the most part when foreigners 'put their foot in it,' they are likely to be seriously upset by unseemly tourist behaviour in temples; wearing a singlet and shorts when visiting a *wat* would be thought very bad taste and you might be asked to leave. Pay attention to any restrictions on photographing inside the *viharn*.

Visitors to temples should remove their shoes before entering the building containing the principal Buddha image. The intention is to show respect to the Buddha, no more, no less; it has nothing to do with the cleansing ritual of Islam. For ordinary people, quite obviously only the shoes can be sensibly removed in order to show respect; it would clearly be quite inappropriate to remove your shirt or blouse, trousers or skirt, so the shoes are (as when entering another house) the obvious means of indicating respect.

When the Prince and Princess of Wales visited the temple of the Emerald Buddha during their visit to Thailand in February 1988, Their Royal Highnesses did not remove their shoes, causing immense consternation among the corps of foreign journalists, but not a ripple of concern among Thai journalists and officials. This was because the Prince of Wales was dressed in a formal western suit, and the Princess appropriately too; and Palace officials noted that His Majesty King Chulalongkorn (Rama V) had decreed earlier this century that if a westerner wished to show respect by visiting a temple (in the tropical heat!) in a western-style suit, that would be respect indeed, as it would look faintly ridiculous for such a person to remove his shoes.

Women are not allowed in the monks' quarters; nor may they hand anything directly to a monk. If an occasion arises, at a religious ceremony for example, where a woman has to present something to a monk, she should place the object on the table or on the ground close to the monk, who will pick it up by himself. Women may, however, speak directly to monks who, in Bangkok at least, are only too keen to practise their English. Women should never touch a monk or his robes.

7

The Thai Language

The Thais mostly came from China and, not surprisingly, their language is related to Chinese. There are many Thai-speaking peoples (known by the generic description 'Tai') living outside the borders of Thailand, including for example Laos, Vietnam, Yunnan in southern China, Burma and as far afield as Assam in northern India.

Thai is at root monosyllabic and tonal; that is, the words consist of one syllable and may be spoken in a variety of tones, low, middle or high, rising or falling. With the arrival of Buddhism in Thailand nearly two thousand years ago, Thai acquired a number of polysyllabic words from the Indian languages Sanskrit and Pali which were non-tonal. For westerners, these polysyllabic words are easier to pronounce and to remember because they are virtually toneless and because some English words are derived from the same Indo-European root as the Thai word, e.g. *buri*/borough meaning town. Thai also took a large number of disyllabic words from Khmer, including many words used in the specialised Thai royal language.

Alphabet

Thai is written from left to right in one continuous stream, without gaps between words and with virtually no punctuation or capital letters. The alphabet is of fairly distant Indian origin and is akin to the Burmese, Lao and Khmer alphabets. There are 44 consonants (but only 28 consonantal sounds), 24 vowels and diphthongs and 4 tone marks (meaning different things for different classes of consonant).

Westerners find it takes a long time to learn to speak or write Thai, and even many of those who have lived most of their lives in Thailand can still only just get by in the spoken language. If it is any consolation, Thais find their own language not all that easy to master.

The written language is mainly a question of intellectual effort. The alphabet needs to be learnt and it is so much more complicated than any western alphabet. Take a few words we have met already:

farang	is written in Thai	'frng' with a above
sanuk	,, ,, ,, ,,	'snk' with u below
bpai tiao	,, ,, ,, ,,	'aibp ito' with a above

Vowels, in short, may be written before, after, above or below the consonant in the same syllable, or in certain combinations of two or three of these positions. This graphic peculiarity takes a long time to absorb. A year's hard study should give you the elements of the alphabet!

Spoken Language

The spoken language is mainly a problem for westerners because of the tones. A simple word may mean several things depending on how it is pronounced:

sua (rising) [pronounced like 'sewer'] means a tiger
sua (falling) means a shirt
sua (low tone) means a mat

Here are some meanings of the sound 'chai,' with various spellings and tones:

fringe	to pass near	to send
end	to use	to pierce
to blow lightly	man	to spend
to glance	to be	to need
to blend	yes	victory

The tone is as important as the spelling of the word. Both must be learnt together. Westerners tend to make the mistake of learning the word first and hoping they will remember the tone later. Thai children learn both word and tone simultaneously. Better to do it their way.

All consonants at the ends of syllables are simplified. When spoken, however they may be spelt, they end only in the hard sounds *p*, *t* and *k* or *m*, *n*, *ng*, *w* and *y*. This is why words ending with an l are pronounced final *n*. 'Oriental Hotel' becomes naturally 'Orientan' and 'Central Department Store' becomes 'Centran.' The word for 'bill,' now used in Thai, is 'bin.' In the spoken language, *ls* and *rs* in non-final position seem interchangeable in Thai and English. Your captain on Thai International will happily wish you, in English, a 'present fright'; do not be alarmed. In Thai, *ls* and *rs* are so intermixed that some purists are complaining that Thai television announcers have developed a fad of using 'rs' for 'ls' and 'ls' for 'rs' quite deliberately.

Forms of Address

Depending on your perceived status and social standing, there are a whole range of personal pronouns in everyday use where in English we use only I/me and you. Safe words are *pom* (men only) and *dichan* (women only) for I/me and *khun* for you (men and women).

Remember to call men and women by their first (given) name. Almost all Thais have a nickname given to them at birth, usually somewhat derogatory like 'Tadpole' and 'Tiny,' designed to ward off malevolent spirits inclined to capture the souls of newly-born infants; these nicknames stay with you all your life and people are very attached to them. Originally, the only names Thais had were first names; family names were introduced comparatively recently earlier this century, many by Royal Decree of King Vajiravudh (Rama VI). First names are generally very much shorter than family names which may have complex Pali or Sanskrit spellings, but are modernised in pronunciation. The polite form of address is *Khun* for both men and women. Thus you would address Mr Suthep Chantavimol as 'Khun Suthep' and his wife Mrs Pranom Chantavimol as 'Khun Pranom'....

Thais, knowing that foreigners find their language almost impossible to learn, will be delighted if you make the effort to say a few words in their language. Here are a few useful phrases:
[*r*=rising, *f*=falling, *l*=low, *h*= high, no sign=even tone]

Vocabulary

khop khun maak[f]	thank you very much
kaw[r] *toht*[f]	sorry, excuse me
mai[f] *dee*	bad, not good
dee maak[f]	very good
yai kern bpai	too big
lek kern bpai	too small
bpai cha cha	go slowly
bpai rew rew	go quickly
trong bpai	go straight on
liew sai[h]	turn left
liew kwaar[r]	turn right
yood tee[f] *nee*[h]	stop here
pood[f] *thai mai*[f] *dai*[f]	I cannot speak Thai
....*yoo*[l] *nai*[r]?	Where is....?
mai[f] *roo*	I don't know (a thing)
mai[f] *ow*	I don't want
prung nee[h]	tomorrow
wan nee[h]	today
mua[f] *waan nee*[h]	yesterday
nung[l]	one
sawng[r]	two
saam[r]	three
see	four
haa[f]	five
hok[l]	six
tjet[l]	seven
bpaet[l]	eight
gkao[f]	nine
sip[l]	ten
sip[l] *et*	eleven
sip[l] *sawng*[r] etc.	twelve
yii sip[l]	twenty
saam[r] *sip*[l] etc.	thirty
nung[l] *roi*[h]	100
nung[l] *pan*	1,000